How to Become Whole without the Better Half

Lou Walker

Outskirts Press, Inc.
Denver, Colorado

The opinions expressed in this manuscript are solely the opinions of the author and do not represent the opinions or thoughts of the publisher. The author represents and warrants that s/he either owns or has the legal right to publish all material in this book.

How to Become Whole without the Better Half
All Rights Reserved.
Copyright © 2008 Lou Walker
v 4.0

Cover Photo © 2008 JupiterImages Corporation. All rights reserved - used with permission.

This book may not be reproduced, transmitted, or stored in whole or in part by any means, including graphic, electronic, or mechanical without the express written consent of the publisher except in the case of brief quotations embodied in critical articles and reviews.

Outskirts Press, Inc.
http://www.outskirtspress.com

ISBN: 978-1-4327-1057-6

Outskirts Press and the "OP" logo are trademarks belonging to Outskirts Press, Inc.

PRINTED IN THE UNITED STATES OF AMERICA

Scriptures were taken from the Holy Bible KJV-King James Version, Royal Publication Inc. Copyright 1964, 1965, 1968.

You are bless to be a blessing!

Lau K Walker
3-15-08

Dedication

This book is dedicated to those who have cried out to God in the name of Jesus for help.

He heard you late in the midnight hour, now He wants to supply your healing power.

He is willing to turn your situation around in the name of Jesus.

This book will be greatly appreciated by any female experiencing the Women at the Well (John 4:7-18).

Remember your tears really are just temporary. May the Lord continue to bless you each and everyday.

Conversation with God

"Before you were born I had plans for your life" (Romans 8:29). I designed you with a blueprint, the Bible for future maintenance and repair. You were suppose to "seek Me and learn of My plans for you" (Deuteronomy 4:29). Sometimes you find time for Me, other times you make decisions without Me.

As I observe your life, there appears a relationship that was formed and cultivated without My guidance. When you met your ex-spouse, where was your relationship with Me? Can you truly say your heart, mind, and soul desired My plans for your life? Originally, I am the one who designed you with plans for your future.

"I knew you before you entered into this world" (Jeremiah 1:5). I formed you while still in the womb of your mother. Though you might deviate away from My plans, I will look forward to your return one day. My plans for your life have been set in stone. When I breathed life into your body, I granted you the ability to make decisions regarding your life here on Earth. Your human design consists of a body, soul, and spirit. "Your body was formed from the dust of the Earth" (Genesis 2:7). I breathed into your nostrils the breath of life and you became a living soul. So I (God) created you in My image, "male and female. He created them according to (Genesis 1:27)." I am reminding you of the beginning because life here on Earth has become so fast. You are forgetting it was because of Me you have arrived here on Earth. Remember I am God, and I do not change (Hebrews 13:8).

I have provided a confirmation of Jesus being My Son for those who have doubts about My deity. My inspired words the Holy Bible provides the following scriptures for your benefit. (Matthew 17 (all), John 5:17-47, Hebrews 1(all)) for starters.

Now I(God) have a question for you, before the age of technology. Which man created for your benefit and can manipulate it when he desires. Who confirm your earthly mother and father as your real (birth) parents? Just thought I would ask since you have problems with My Son. **I am that I am**, Holy, Righteous, Spiritual and the Living God who never slumbers or

How to Become Whole without the Better Half

sleep. The **DNA** you find in your body was provided by Me. No man has the ability to manipulate your DNA. I just thought, I would remind you of My marvelous work.

Try to remember not to entertain foolish questions about My deity. (2 Timothy 2:23, Psalm 14 and 53 (all), Proverbs 19:3, 1 Corinthians 1:18) provides insight from past generations before you were born. Jesus Christ provided you a helper to guide you regarding spiritual things. The guidance of the Holy Spirit provides wisdom, knowledge and understanding about spiritual things.

I (God) have sent My Son Jesus to live here on Earth. So you might observe His life while being obedient to Me your Father in Heaven. After teaching and training future leaders, My Son gave up His life on Earth to cover the sins of man. My Son, Jesus, now resides at My right side, being a mediator between you and Me (God). He continuously informs Me of situations where I need to have mercy and dispense My grace to My children on Earth. Dear children on Earth accept the fact that you cannot come to know Me unless My spirit draws your spirit unto Me. Remember I am a spirit (John 4:24) and the spirit must speak to the spirit in order to be drawn to God. We do not make decisions to accept God unless the spirit within us is drawn by God who is a spirit (John 6:44). The spirit of God speaks to the spirit imparted to you, in order for you to be in communication with the living God (1 Corinthians 3:16). According to Genesis (6:3) "My spirit will not always strive with man because he is also flesh." Jesus' arrival here on earth allows us to be enlightened by the Holy Spirit.

Providing we desire a personal relationship with Him. We can pray for wisdom, knowledge and understanding according to (Ephesians 1:15-19), you must be ready to receive the words of God as the truth.

According to the scripture when a male and female choose a marriage covenant with God, the two become one. When we choose a mate for marriage, we are no longer two separate individuals. According to (1 Corinthians 6:16-18), "the two becomes one." "Your soul binds with the person you became intimate with (sexual encounter)." If this was not your first experience, you have bonded with many souls, which cause you great confusion. According to scripture, we were not designed to test the marriage bed before marriage. God's plan for your life consists of one soul mate. The other sexual encounters we allow cause much confusion. We now have something to measure and compare, which never was the original plan for those created in Gods image. This confusion of your soul is the immaterial part of man and leaves the body at death. "I gave you your soul and it belongs to Me (God)" (Genesis 35:18, Ezekiel 18:3-4). "Remember the spirit also leaves the body at death" (Ecclesiastes 12:7). "You can tie your soul to man but your spirit is a part of God without binds or ties to man." Many find themselves with their souls tied to others in a form of bondage.

Notes/Questions

Obedience

God is willing to loose those bonds, when you are ready to surrender your life to Him, by choosing a life of obedience to the Father, Son, and the Holy Spirit. God will observe your heart, when you are ready to be released. Your mind will always say yes, but your heart will say no. This confusion sends you back into the relationship continuously until you are ready to cry out to God sincerely. He will observe your heart and acknowledge you are ready to cut the ties for this relationship. Therefore we need to stop and think about the person we presented to God for a future mate. Did we really, earnestly consult God regarding His plans for their life? Did we assume this person was the one He designed for us?

According to the inspired words of God His, plans are for peace and not confusion. (John 3:16-21) "The one you presented to God as a future mate should not have answered the call as a soul mate for you." He has sent His Son so you could have peace here on Earth. (John

13:17). Your decision has caused you much pain. He has seen your tears and heard your prayers. His words to you are "I love you and will never forsake you in times of trouble." As you take the time to reference Me, you should always reflect on My love, which surpasses all understanding.

What you fail to understand about male and females can be found in Deuteronomy 22:29, "Any male that participates in a sexual act with a woman is removing a part of her by humbling her." According to My plans, the guidelines for husband and wife this procedure is normal. Problems begin to present themselves, when the mate (male) removes himself from being a companion to his wife. Remember the day you went before Me (God) requesting My blessing for this marriage covenant. We will not bring up those who chose to bypass My blessings and seek a Justice of the Peace.

Many of you are hurt and angry with Me (God). Why? Did you love Me more than the person you chose as your better half? I do not think this is true; I am aware of your thoughts and actions before they take place.

How to Become Whole without the Better Half

You did not recognize that this person was not in the plans that I (God) had for your life. A relationship with this person constantly causes pain and heartache, because of your disobedience to Me. I would like to restore that part of you taken when you were married. Come in repentance of your disobedience with the marriage covenant or testing of the marriage bed without a marriage covenant with Me. Jesus', conversation with the woman at the well, "Go call your husband" (John 4:6-19). Jesus talks about the water that will never run dry. This lady had five husbands and was currently with another gentleman. If you have experienced this many relationships trying to find your soul mate, it is time for some spiritual assistance. Jesus speaks of the husbands the woman had; we send them away because they are not fulfilling our thirst. Jesus has come so He might quench your thirst; Jesus said he who believes in Me would not thirst. Until we have a sincere relationship with Jesus, we will always thirst for someone else. Everything you need Jesus is willing to supply making you whole in all things. Jesus would like you to totally surrender your life to Him, in order for you to become whole again. Jesus will provide for all your needs as long as He is the center of your life. For those who have tried, to have an

Lou Walker

honest relationship with the better half. Only to find they were not capable of pleasing the other half. Jesus is willing to help and carry you when you are torn and weary. Just be willing to love Him like your first love on Earth.

When you ask in the name of Jesus, He will do more than you can begin to imagine.

Restoring the missing part:

Anytime you desire to become whole with the loss of the better half. Remember this can only be accomplished by having a personal relationship with Me your Father, who resides in Heaven (John 4:24). First you must understand I am Holy and a Spirit. If you read My words, My instructions are you must come through My Son Jesus before having a relationship with Me. I need you to understand I am Holy (John 4:24). In Leviticus 20:7, we must remember to "Sanctify yourselves therefore and be ye holy: I am the Lord your God and ye shall keep My status and do them, I am the Lord which sanctify you." God allowed some people to come before Him (Exodus 28:35,43,29:20), before Jesus arrival as His Son. They were required to meet certain requirements before coming into the presence of God. Aaron's sons Nadab and Abihu did not understand the holiness of God. They made the mistake of bringing an offering to God without following the procedures given to their father Aaron. God did not hesitate to remove them from the land of the living.

Lou Walker

They died for their disobedience to God (Numbers 3:4). Maybe you still do not understand God's holiness. Read (Leviticus 10:6) if you feel that God is not fair. He warned Aaron and his other sons not to grieve for those who desired to dishonor Him; remember He is God and Holy. When we think about the President of the United States, can we actually come into his presence when we feel like it? The answer is no and do not think about seeing the President without an appointment. However, we want access to the Father who resides in Heaven; it is necessary to start with His Son Jesus Christ. Only through the Son will you gain a relationship with the Father.

Best Teacher

We are all sinners saved by God's grace and mercy. God decided the only way we could have a relationship with Him was for Him to live among us. He imparted Himself to a virgin by the name of Mary (Luke 1:26-38). He arrived as the Son Jesus Christ in the flesh. He lived and dwelled among sinners without sinning while living here on Earth. His purpose on Earth was to teach and train those who desired to know the Father. He provided a way out of living a life of sin (Romans 6(all)). We should pray the following prayer with a sincere heart.

Notes/Questions

Sinners Prayer

Dear God I am a sinner. I am so very sorry for all my sins (omission and unknowns). Please forgive me of all my unrighteousness. I sincerely believe you sent your Son, Jesus to live among us. I believe in the birth, life, death, resurrection, and ascension of your Son Jesus Christ. Father I pray you take control of my life and make me one of your servants here on Earth. I pray for the anointing of the Holy Spirit upon my life. Lord, as others look at my life I pray they would see Jesus and desire to know Him as their personal Lord and savior, Father. I ask all these blessings in the name of Jesus, amen.

God has asked His children to keep His commandments and accept His Son Jesus Christ. So we might have a personal relationship with Him as our Heavenly Father.

If we can keep the scripture found in (Matthew 22:37-40). These two commandments actually, cover the Ten Commandments given to Moses for God's chosen people the Israelites. We just need to accept our helper provided by Jesus the guidance of the Holy Spirit for success.

There is something about the name of Jesus. He removes all burdens you are willing to lay at his feet. Sometime we say in our mind, we would like to give up certain situations. God looks at our heart and observes our actions reminding us. The mind says yes, but the heart is saying no. He is patiently waiting, as you struggle to free your heart from the situation. He is willing to carry you through the storms of life. We must remember, without Christ you are like a ship tossed and driven. The Holy Spirit will lead us, knowing with Jesus Christ the Lord will make a way somehow.

Your anchor will always hold in the name of Jesus. Remember if Jesus can calm the sea making the waves behave (Matthew 8:23-27). Exactly which storm in your life seems to be out of control? Put all your trust in Jesus and allow Him to restore the half of you, which you gave up in your marriage covenant. Only through Jesus Christ, you can become whole again without the better half. Jesus is willing and able to carry you through the storms of life. Regardless of the circumstances or situations presented to you.

A New Beginning

The day you become tired and broken-hearted you will be on your way to a life with a new beginning. There was a woman presented to Jesus for committing adultery by her accusers. He just stooped and began to write on the ground; whatever He wrote caused her accusers to flee. When He looked up He asked "where are your accusers?" She said "there are not any He told her to go and sin no more (John 8:7-11)." When you receive your release from the old to become new, Jesus will restore that part removed during your marriage covenant. This can only be accomplished when you are ready to surrender your life to Jesus Christ and make Him the Lord of your life. Rest assured the next marriage covenant you participate in must be a threesome. A husband who desires to become spiritually mature, Jesus Christ, will be the mediator (1Timothy 2:5) and a wife who desire to grow spiritually. There is no failure in this formula. Then we will be crucified with Christ; it is not I who live but Jesus who lives through me.

Lou Walker

As Christians, we need to acknowledge God has an order for all things. He created a Son for our benefit (1 John 2:20-27). He provided love and compassion for those created in His image. He realizes we would never have that personal relationship needed to relate to Him as a Father except He models the life needed to relate to Him in the Spirit. We must remember God is Holy and a Spirit; we are humans with a spirit. Only by the guidance of the Holy Spirit we will be allowed to communicate with the living God. He can speak to the spirit within you (1 Corinthians 3:16) and (John 4:24). Those who truly know the Father, Son and Holy Spirit will always acknowledge God as a Spirit.

When we refuse to accept God's Son Jesus Christ, we are not allowed to have a relationship with the Father. Why can't we have a relationship with the Father? Because He is Holy and spiritual and we are merely humans. The spirit understands spiritual communication (1 John 4:1-6). This is why we need a relationship with the Son, Jesus Christ. Jesus speaks to the Father who is Holy and a Spirit on our behalf (Romans 8:34). Remember the words of Jesus when He ascended into Heaven? This is your helper the Holy Spirit (Acts 2(all)).

The problem:

According to scripture, anytime a man has sexual contact with a woman she becomes the weaker vessel (Deuteronomy 21:14, 22:24, 29, 1Peter 3:7). "Before Christ you were stoned for giving up your virginity" (Deuteronomy 22:20-21). Because of the birth, life, death, resurrection, and ascension of Jesus surely we do not want to play the whore according to scripture (Deuteronomy 22:21), remember you were humbled. Jesus has come so you might have life more abundantly. Choosing to be disobedient allows you to suffer the consequences for your continuous rebellion (1 John 3:5-10). Jesus taught us while living here on earth the expectations of each generation. They should leave a foundation of truth for the next generation (Hebrews 10:26-31).

As we look around in the twenty-first century, you have more divorces than marriages; has anyone stopped and asked why? If a male or female has sexual relations outside of marriage, according to scripture, they are being disobedient and will suffer consequences. Experiencing sex with someone other than your marriage partner will set you up for a failed marriage. A human has a spiritual and natural (flesh) body, because you are human and operating in the flesh (1 Corinthians 15:42-52). Every encounter will be measured against the one you thought was the best. The problem with this disaster is you will never be satisfied as long as you have something to compare.

I believe everyone has a soul mate; remember how Job waited on the Lord? David also reminds us to wait on God (Psalm 27:14). Tell me why you cannot wait again. One day while listen to the teaching of Chuck Swindoll he spoke about Corrie Ten Boom not being married. You might have a situation like Corrie Ten Boom. "God called her husband, but he never answered the call." Look around at this current generation. Do you think we have our own agendas and personal gods requiring our attention?

We need to be obedient and wait on the one who was originally designed for you. God will send your spouse and you will be guaranteed a match made in Heaven. God never designed you as a square to fit in a round hole. If we are going to change the generational curse of divorce, it must start with you. Once you have been restored, you can teach your daughters, sisters, aunts and nieces to strive to become whole without the better half. Encourage them to never test the marriage bed without a marriage covenant with God, in the name of Jesus.

Notes/Questions

Sex outside Marriage:

We should not be deceived in this generation according to the words of God. Men and women will not be satisfied with God's original plan: for the marriage bed. They will burn with desire to gain more satisfaction with each other (Romans 1:26-32). The Bible states anytime bodily fluids are released from a male or female (Leviticus 15:16-33). They should be respected and maintained according to His words found in Leviticus.

Some of us have accepted oral sex as a form of needed foreplay, before a sexual encounter. We really need to count the cost of encountering all these body fluids before finding your soul mate.

Only God knows the disadvantage we allow ourselves to experience by consuming fluids not designed for consumption.

If you have never experienced this activity then the message is not for you. We have a genera-

Lou Walker

tion of people who are making the rules as they go through life. They need to know the truth when things begin to fall apart around them. They should reflect on their lifestyle and consider the cost.

We always have the option of believing and receiving or ignoring and experiencing the consequences according to God's inspired words the Bible.

There were generations before ours who chose to respect and honor the words of God.

They did not deal with the many health issues we have available today. We are also causing many of our health problems as well as those suffered by our children because of our disobedience. Check the health statistics from past generations and compare them to this present generation; there is a difference.

We are more technically advanced in the medical field, believing we can fix things without spiritual guidance. This is not the answer when we choose a life of disobedience according to the words of God. Bandages' cannot cover injuries requiring stitches'. The healing process is greater than just covering it for a little while expecting the healing to take place.

We are not the first generation with medical science trying to heal without the power of God. Jesus provides the divine healing source in this generation.

Reading Psalm 106 (All) insight is provided regarding the Israelites sin and their refusal of Gods Love.

There was a time women actually wore a chastity belt to maintain their virginity. You might laugh but this was one of the ways used to help females stay virgins until they were married. They did not have to worry about becoming a weaker person to a male who was not their husband.

According to scripture, a male can humble a female. She should only participate in sexual activity with a male design to make her complete, which would be her husband. This is why the two shall become one; he will complete what he has taken from her.

Some women are experiencing heartache and pain without knowing the source of their hurting. They are not aware of the fact; they are dealing with five of the deadly sins very often without realizing the reason. Could it be because they are experiencing a feeling of being incomplete? Sometime women are dealing with anger and they do not understand why they are so angry. Envious of others, lying, gluttony and greed these are five of the seven deadly sins according to scripture (Proverbs 6:16-19). There are also warnings against adultery (Proverbs 6:20-35 and Matthews 5:31-32).

If you are divorced and need a husband you should reference (Isaiah 54:5-8). "The maker is your husband and the Lord of host." "The woman who desires someone else husband" should read (Proverbs 7:1-5). God speaks to men on how to avoid women traps. The woman of the twenty-first century needs to make sure she is not fulfilling scripture found in (Proverbs 7:10-27). God's warning to men, regarding the woman that destroys a man. Men have been warned without the guidance of the Holy Spirit. A woman has the power to break a man's spirit (Proverb 6:26). She needs to understand his revenge will be like a bull in a China store. Christian women should avoid being this type of woman (Proverbs 9:13-18). Heaven help those males being trained by a female without spiritual guidance and male input. They will have all the characteristics of a female with the capabilities of destroying a woman presented in (Proverbs 5-7). Women need to also understand some men desire to be evil according to Proverb 2(all). There is a word from God reminding them to listen to wisdom and not the evils being presented to them.

Listen to the words of the wisest man created by God who still fell into temptation with women. Learn from his mistakes (Proverbs 10-15). Teachings on right and wrong, wise and foolish are contrasted. Do we need guidance from God regarding what things are moral, ethical, and spiritual standards? (Proverbs 16-24) "When man's ways please the Lord he makes even his enemies to be at peace with him (Proverbs 16:7)." "It is okay not to have all the answers" (Proverbs 17:28).

The following scripture reveals God is not pleased with those who choose to fornicate (Act 15:20). Paul speaks to the Gentiles saying fornication (participate in sexual activity outside the marriage covenant with God) is to be abstained (1 Corinthians 6:18). There is still unity among those who choose to follow the guidance of the Holy Spirit. Regardless of the World's influence in the twenty-first century (1

Lou Walker

John 2:7-17) reminds us to continue to trust in the words of the living God. There are some women who are not **desperate housewives.** They acknowledge I (God) can provide for **all My children.** The guidance of the Holy Spirit reveals to them they only need **one life to live** according to My words in the Bible. They should never spend time in the **General Hospital** for hurt and pain. My Son is their healing source. They realize with guidance from the Holy Spirit, they will always be **bold and beautiful.** God expects us to follow His guidelines for marriage and divorce found in the Bible. (1 Thessalonians 4:3) "This is the will of God that you should abstain from fornication."

We have been told to protect our minds in (Isaiah 26:3-4) "speaks of how we will be kept in perfect peace whose minds are stayed on the Father who resides in Heaven." If we do not protect our minds others will influence your thoughts and decisions in this generation. There is a spiritual battle more powerful than we can begin to comprehend for our thoughts and decisions. We really do not wrestle with flesh and blood according to (Ephesians 6:11-20). We need to put on the whole armor of the living God and recognize the battle is not ours it really belongs to the Lord.

Possible Consequences for Sex outside of Marriage:

We are humans created in the image of the living God. We should thank God for allowing us to make decisions and not creating robots in this generation. The only problems with having choices are being required to make decisions. When you do not have prior knowledge, you find yourself experiencing consequences for not making the right decisions. Anytime we decide to experiment with sexual encounters outside the marriage covenant with God. (Proverb 14:12) reminds us of the consequences. This twenty-first century generation has experienced some hard times for following the world's advice about sexual encounters. The consequences sometimes are AIDS, HIV, HPV or any other STDS. God has not allowed man to provide a vaccine to cure our disobedience as of today. It really is possible to cause your own health problems or sentence yourself to death; without the guidance of the Holy Spirit. The world tries to encourage your thoughts but they are not allowed to heal your hurt and pain. Remember God has patience with those who are without prior knowledge, but those who have prior knowledge and refuse to accept the inspired words of God as the truth (Romans 2:8).

Our only **hope** is for God to have mercy in the name of Jesus (Titus 1:2), without this **hope** our lives will be shorten among the land of the living.

Heaven help those who share their love by having sexual encounters in this generation. *They* will silence two friends and *they* will silence two friends and so on and so on. Until we now have an epidemic in the area of HPV, HIV and AIDS among some races.

 Please do not become angry with God about your decisions in life. This will only delay the healing process if He desires to heal you in Jesus' name.

We should accept the consequences without blaming others for our mistakes. Anytime we humble ourselves with a broken spirit unto God in Jesus name: deciding to confess our sin and ask forgiveness in the name of Jesus. These will be steps taken in the right direction (1 John 3:5-10).

Whether our choices are good or bad, we need to remember it was our decision to make the choice. Through Jesus Christ, our sins are forgiven. If God so desires, we can be healed in the name of Jesus. Remember we made the decision to sin against God, now it is His time to make a decision regarding our health. He already knows if we will go and sin no more with the guidance of the Holy Spirit, or continue to make wrong choices grieving the Spirit of God.

If we are dealing with any of the seven deadly sins: greed, pride, lying, envy, anger, gluttony, or slothfulness (Proverbs 6:16-19). We must bring them before God in Jesus name, laying them at the feet of Jesus refusing to access them again.

Do you think a relationship with someone outside the will of God's plans, is worth a possible death sentence?

It is time to stop justifying our need to fornicate. The scripture states if the desire is that strong we should consider marriage (1 Corinthians 7:8-9).

Notes/Questions

Lord how can my life be changed?

We need to accept that God designed us with a blueprint, the Bible. If we read the blueprint, we will learn of the necessary tools needed for functioning in the twenty-first century. When a person designs a house a blueprint must be provided regarding future plans. Any steps taken outside the original design will cause problems. Anytime we lose our direction regarding Gods original plans for our life. We must be able to reference the original starting place, in order for us to get back on track. We must obtain the original instructions and design for our life here on earth. Some of us have never been on track regarding Gods plans and purpose, so it will be difficult to tell if you are off track. God's word, the Bible, is man's blueprint for a successful life here on Earth. If you are currently struggling to be freed from the sins listed in (Colossians 3:6-11). It is possible your spiritual life needs some spiritual substance. Try finding some quiet time praying and studying the Holy Bible with the guidance of the Holy Spirit. Remember a natural (flesh) understanding can

Lou Walker

not comprehend things spiritually provided. Only by the guidance of the Holy Spirit, we will obtain spiritual growth. The Holy Spirit is willing to release you from anything you are willing to give up here on earth (Matthew 16:19). Sometimes we by pass all the warnings God provide to change our ways. We do a 360 degree turn when God is expecting a 180 degree turn from us. We force the hand of God to get our attention, and then we get mad for experiencing consequences for being disobedient. We must acknowledge the test provided in (1 John 1:5-10) instructs us regarding light and darkness. There is a great difference (1 John 2:1-6) reminds us of our help which comes from Jesus to maintain the light. **Hey who moved?** The living God who resides in Heaven did not, check your position again? Anything freely given up requires less pain and hurt for the children of the living God.

Solution #1: The obvious solution to the problem is to start teaching one generation at a time. It is time to teach each female about the consequences, of being disobedient for having sexual encounters before marriage. Help each one to fully understand how she loses a part of her self-worth, which can never be replaced without Jesus Christ. Explain how each sexual encounter makes her feel weak and vulnerable. She loses the ability to lead others without the guidance of the Holy Spirit. If God really speaks through you as a leader, you are guaranteed to be successful in leadership.

According to (Isaiah 55:11) His words spoken through you shall not return void but shall accomplish that which pleases Him. God's words will always prosper when He sends them forth. This can only take place in the spirit, so you must have spiritual guidance from the Holy Spirit in Jesus name. Those who hear the words of God will be able to receive His words and glorify Him in Jesus' name.

According to (1 Peter 3:7) the wife represents the weaker vessel. The husband's prayer life is hindered for his disobedience also. She needs to realize continuous sexual encounters for the female appear to hurt more than the males. He takes a part of her each time and she will never regain her loss without total submission to Jesus Christ.

Solution #2: It is hard, sometimes to accept that men and women are different when it comes to sexual encounters. Most women will totally disagree with that statement. Reading Deuteronomy (22:29) provides insight to the warning provided for women. God never said the man would be humbled. He said the female would experience this weakened state. Who are we, to question the warning God provided before you were even born? Remember God knew the decisions we were going to make while He formed us in our mother's womb. We have been given a fork in the road. Anytime we choose to have a relationship with the Father, Son, and the Holy Spirit. We will receive wisdom, knowledge, and understanding with the guidance of the Holy Spirit. "A relationship with Jesus gives you peace in the midst of all storms" (John 14:27) but choices without spiritual guidance causes much heartache and pain.

Solution #3: Let's start each day as a new day. Start by removing all things. Read Psalm 51. Always remember where the spirit of the Lord is there is liberty (2 Corinthians 3: 17-18).

> Surrender to Jesus this day.
> Empty yourself of all things.
> Love the Lord in Song and praise.
> Fill me Lord this day with your Holy Spirit.

It is going to be a great day and thank God for it! You have your health and strength and you

How to Become Whole without the Better Half

know you have been redeemed by the blood of the lamb! On this day I will not whine I will shine!

Solution #4: When you believe in the Father, Son, and the Holy Spirit you will be empowered by the Holy Spirit, as long as you allow Jesus to lead and you follow his leadership (Romans 8(All)). You will be given the strength to do all things through Christ, who strengthens you with the guidance of the Holy Spirit. Every decision you make will be pleasing to the Father who resides in Heaven (Philippians 4:13).

Solution #5: Communicate the vision of becoming whole without the better half. Jesus' conversation He held with the woman at the well (John 4:7-18), usually causes others to think. He was advising her of the problems she had with marrying all those men. They were not the answer; she needed a relationship with Him. Jesus is the only one to replace all that was taken by your better half.

Jesus' teaching on divorce is in (Matthew 19:5-6). How many of us can honestly say when we said our wedding vows we cut the ties with our parental influence on our lives? Matthew (19:5) states this was a necessary step, choosing to ignore the warning cause's disobedience. The marriage should have been a threesome for success. Husband, Christ, and the wife anybody else permitted in this decision-making can create a disaster. We need to evaluate our relationships with our parents until it is fully understood, they **must** release their control over your life. Marriage should be avoided at all costs. The hurt and pain provided in a divorce will be more costly without understanding God's words. Anytime you can have an honest mediator (Christ Jesus), you can weather any storm of life (1Timothy 2:5).

Please do not plead ignorance:

According to (Hosea 4:6) God reminds Israel "My people are destroyed for lack of knowledge." We usually reject the unknown. We shall be reminded if we reject Him; He shall reject our future generations and us. If we stop and look around this is taking place today among the younger generations. They are perishing because they lack the knowledge of the Father, Son, and the Holy Spirit. According to Hosea (4:10) "they shall eat and not have enough." Do we have a problem with people not being satisfied in this generation? We are over weight and seek perverted sexual interest in this day and time? "Daughters will commit whoredom and spouses will commit adultery" (Hosea 4:13-14). Do we see this taking place today? What are we giving up for God and still being disobedient? According to (Hosea, 6:6) God desire is for you to know His word and choose a life of obedience over the things you sacrifice for Him.

God will begin to make necessary changes for

those who choose disobedience instead of the plans He has for our life. The consequence will be greater than we expect. When He calls us into obedience, we need to reach those in disobedience to do His will. Choosing to answer God's call helps the person being called and those who are being disobedient. If the older women would take the time and teach the younger women then, every generation would learn of God's expectation for women. Any past mistakes can be used for personal and spiritual growth for each generation.

A continuation of generational divorces is very displeasing to God. He expects a generation to stop and consult Him regarding His plans for their life. We can observe Israel's struggle with obedience and the consequences they faced for disobedience in the Old Testament. We should learn from their mistakes and observe the consequences they faced during their generation. Choosing to live a life of obedience allows the Father to bless His children in the name of Jesus.

Our blessings in life will only be received because of our obedience to the Father, Son, and the Holy Spirit. There is always the possibility of a generation, not being interested in

How to Become Whole without the Better Half

God's plan. Their disobedience will allow them to suffer the consequences, just like past generations found in the Bible. As soon as the next generation chooses a life of obedience things will turn around for them. They will experience God's blessings allowing them to have peace, which surpasses all of mans natural (Textbooks and common sense) understanding (Philippians 4:7).

(1 Corinthians 6:15-20) we are reminded of our bodies belonging to God. Every sin we commit is outside the body until we choose to fornicate or have an adulterous relationship. The Holy Spirit resides inside the body and accepts sexual encounters as being a part of the marriage covenant. Anything presented outside of the marriage covenant with God is unacceptable. Maybe you are experiencing (Lamentations 1:2) after Jerusalem refused to be obedient to the words of God. He finally afflicted her for the multitude of her transgressions (1:5b). The scripture speaks of what Zion experienced for being disobedient. We need to remove Zion and make this personal so we can relate to this situation. Until we experience a broken spirit, we will always find ourselves calling for lovers when they have deceived us. Surely this sounds familiar to someone, who has

tried without success to walk away and never look back.

We should take the time and reflect on a female, fighting a battle with health concerns because of sexual disobedience. Ladies this is a serious matter; it is time out for suffering unnecessarily. A genuine relationship with Jesus can turn things around for you or any female who chooses to call on the name of Jesus. When you take the time to reference the words of God, you will personally begin to receive a spiritual healing from the inside out. God will start with your heart and a light will shine so others might see His glory.

Anytime you find yourself being tempted to indulge in sexual activity, without a marriage covenant with God. **Stop** and start crying unto your Father who resides in Heaven and loves His children (Psalm 107:13-21). Listen to the words of David, when he cried unto the Lord during his distress (Psalm 142). Jesus will pick you up and hold you until you regain your inner strength. How many times have a child cried and you stopped whatever you were doing to comfort them? This is exactly how Jesus intercedes on our behalf to the Father in Heaven. When you fall, He is there to pick you

How to Become Whole without the Better Half

up dust you off and set you back on the right road.

Read (Romans 8-10) and be encouraged regarding your relationship with a Father who really cares for you.

Notes/Questions

The reason something must be done now!

We are suffering the consequences of our continuous sinful behaviors in this generation, without the guidance of the Holy Spirit. Many have health problems and children who refuse to be obedient. Our love for them is so great until their rebellion will send you to an early grave. We must learn to accept, we are only given a certain number of years to influence their lives here on earth. We need to teach and train those God entrusted to us about His plans and purpose for their lives. We need to release them to God and continue to pray for them in the name of Jesus. When they submit to peer- pressure, we need to make sure we are committed to prayer in Jesus' name.

The Holy Spirit will always speak to you as a child of the living God, in the name of Jesus. Anytime we are ready to be still and listen, the Holy Spirit will never compete for your time. We will be provided with the guidance to go and sin no more. Just as Jesus told, the woman brought to Him to be stoned for committing adultery.

Lou Walker

The scripture speaks of waiting on God and how He will wipe all of our tears away (Isaiah 25:8, Revelation 7:17). "Those who wait we will be glad and rejoice in His salvation" (Isaiah 25:8-9). Remember weeping might endure for a night but joy comes with the morning light (Psalm 30:5).

A reason to become whole without the better half is found in (Songs of Solomon 8:6-7). If you love someone more than Jesus, departing from this person can be stronger than death. It is possible for you to think life is not worth living without this relationship. Love can appear very powerful without Jesus Christ. We really need spiritual guidance to be released from this kind of love. This can only be accomplished by having a relationship with the Father, Son, and the Holy Spirit.

Those who have been through a broken marriage covenant with God know the pain can be like childbirth but is not so easily forgotten. There's a constant reminder without Christ, you feel a part of you is missing and you are no longer complete. You must have a relationship with God, our Father who resides in Heaven through Jesus His Son. This relationship allows you regain that which was taken and be restored in the name of Jesus.

When you have a relationship with Jesus the scriptures in (Isaiah 26:12-14) has meaning. You realize God does provide peace in times of need. All those other gods are removed and calling on the name of Jesus becomes automatic in times of trouble. We will find they are dead and shall not rise for they have been destroyed.

How many of us are able to understand the scripture? When it speaks of a trial being like a woman giving birth to a child she cries out because of the depth of her pain. Yet, when she looks on the child, the pain is usually forgotten.

When we choose to be disobedient, refusing to follow the truth, according to the inspired words found in the Bible. We will also experience pain in the form of consequences. Anytime we have hidden the word of God within our hearts. The pain can be removed at a greater pace because you have a mediator in Christ. He asked the Father to have mercy on you His child (providing you are a child of God).

Notes/Questions

Beauty

When God gives favor to women who are born with beauty, they must acknowledge this blessing is from Him.

Anytime a woman chooses a relationship without the Father, Son, and the Holy Spirit, we will all observe her beauty as a fading flower. Remember the scripture states the Lord gives and the Lord takes it away. Bless it be the name of the Lord (Job 1:21). Any flower without living water will dry up and fade away. Mothers need to remind those daughters who have an abundance of beauty, unless they take the time and glorify God for His blessing. They will become like a dried rose very soon. Jesus is the living water, God speaks to Jerusalem regarding being blessed and carrying on with other nations outside of His will. "She is carrying herself like an imperious whore" (Ezekiel 16:30). He reminds Jerusalem of the proverb which says "as is the mother so is the daughter." They will repeat or copy your action (Ezekiel 16:44). Mothers in this generation really need to become lights for

Lou Walker

their daughters. Some females with outer beauty struggle with low self-esteem, when others think they have high self-esteem. They do not have the inner strength others possess without physical beauty. This is why; physical beauty can become a curse instead of a blessing without spiritual guidance. They should be taught beauty and brains can coexist with the guidance of the Holy Spirit.

Sons and Daughters:

Because the Lord is your shepherd you really do have everything you need. He has ac knowledged, those with a personal relationship with the Father, Son and the Holy Spirit are accepted as His children. Just like He acknowledge Israel in (Jeremiah 31:1, 9) (2 Corinthians 6:16-18). We are the sons and daughters of a Holy, Spiritual, Righteous and Living God who resides in Heaven (John 1:12, Galatians 3:24-29, 4:4-7 Romans 8:14-17, Ephesians 1:5). Only by the guidance of the Holy Spirit, we are allowed to have this personal relationship with the living God in Heaven. The natural mind can not relate to things inspired by God (1 Corinthians 15: 20-58). They will always appear foolish to someone without the guidance of the Holy Spirit. This is why, we should not be unequally yoke (2 Corinthians 6:14) in marriage. (1 Corinthians 7:16) Paul said those who are married should not leave their spouse. It is possible they might observe your life and become a believer. We need to give Paul credit for this statement not the Lord Jesus Christ. The

Lou Walker

Lord said if you are burning with passion and can not contain your desire for the opposite sex "it is better to marry than to burn (1 Corinthians 7: 9-11)." If the wife leaves her husband she should remain unmarried unless she goes back to her first husband. The husband is not allowed to leave his wife. Paul speaks about remarriage for the man and woman according to Gods inspired word the Bible (1 Corinthians 7: 27-40).

Remember there is a physical and spiritual death humans can experience while living here on earth. God observes our heart and knows our thoughts before we make any decision. Do not pull the "**I thought he was the one**" card. The Holy Spirit is willing to lead as long as you are willing to follow, His guidance for your soul mate. The flesh (physical body) will guaranteed you another divorce with more pain, hurt and sorrow in the future. Surely you do not want to hear the words from Jesus "go call your husband because the one you are currently with is not your husband (John 4:7-18)."

We have been warned from past generations "The soul that sins shall die" (Ezekiel 18:4). If a man be just and choose a life of obedience regarding the words of God. Then, he shall surely live verse (6-31) provides detail of sins displeasing to God, which causes death. (Ezekiel 18:32) God receives no pleasure when Israel sinned with the consequences of death. Can we learn from past generations mistakes in this day and time? Shall we also be like Israel and not please God?

Notes/Questions

Levels of Spiritual Growth

The Holy Spirit revealed Himself to me when I began to grow spiritually. There were different levels of spiritual maturity as you grow spiritually you begin to understand spiritual guidance. Just because we faithfully attended church every Sunday, spiritual growth is not guaranteed. We must find time to study the words of God with the guidance of the Holy Spirit. We really need down time and quiet time without interruptions. We also must be still and allow the Holy Spirit to speak to us. The wisdom, knowledge and understanding provided allow you to grow spiritually (Exodus 31:3). (1 Corinthians 3:1-3) speaks of a carnal mind hindering spiritual growth.

(Isaiah 28:9) describes who shall lead God's people when questions are asked. When the elders of Israel came to question God, He had a problem with them because of their rebellion. He asked them, "Are ye come to inquire of me?" As I live, says the Lord God "I will not be inquired of by you" (Ezekiel 20:30-31). Children

Lou Walker

of God need to choose a life of obedience in the name of Jesus. Acknowledging Jesus as our mediator, and He is willing to speak on our behalf anytime we desire to question God. We need to humbly go in the name of Jesus acknowledging the guidance of the Holy Spirit (Ezekiel 20:31). God did not allow Israel to question Him, when they chose to be disobedient regarding His words. He expects us to follow His order of communication provided by Him through His Son, Jesus Christ also.

Trusting Idols and not God

The same warnings given to Egypt are applied, for those who choose to be disobedient in the twenty-first century (Isaiah 31:3). He said Egyptians are men and not God. "The horses are flesh not spirit." When the Lord shall stretch out His hand those who help and hope without His guidance they shall fail. God is speaking of Judah, is there a reason in this generation we cannot learn from their mistakes.

(Isaiah 33:22) "We must remember the Lord is our judge, the lord is our lawgiver, and the Lord is our King He will save us:" in the name of Jesus . (Isaiah 35:3-10) reminds us we can be restored by having a relationship with our Lord and Savior.

There is a warning for the twenty-first century in (Isaiah 34:16). We need to find time to read with the guidance of the Holy Spirit. Only then will you understand, that you will receive inner strength and renewal from the Holy Spirit. We can encourage others who fear, honor and re-

Lou Walker

spect the living God. To be strong and know the Lord He is God. Then we will see and hear things according to the inspired words of God.

We need to accept the facts; Jesus is a rock in a weary land, a shelter in the mist of a storm. He is also water in a dry place reference (Isaiah 32:2-3). God's speaks a warning to the women in Jerusalem (32:9-11). He speaks of the many ways for them to avoid trouble. He warns us to always listen to His voice and hear His speech. We should always be mindful of God in times of trouble. Choosing a relationship without Him will cause much pain and sorrow. We <u>must</u> have spiritual guidance from Him. This can only be accomplished by having a relationship with His Son Jesus Christ. Remember Jesus had to return to His Father in order for us to receive our helper, the Holy Spirit.

(Isaiah 33:6) we must remember wisdom and knowledge shall always be our foundation. We shall always have the guidance of the Holy Spirit as long, as we choose to be obedient to God who resides in Heaven. Anytime we choose not to be obedient to God, according to His will. We become like grass in the field experiencing Texas heat without living waters. Does anyone know what happens to grass in

Texas heat? The grass withes and flowers fade but the words of God shall stand forever (Isaiah 40:7-8). We really need the guidance of the Holy Spirit to stand forever. Jesus will carry you according to (Isaiah 40:11). Be sure and ask the Father to lead you comfort strengthen and keep you. Jesus is willing and able He will carry you through (1 Corinthians 3:11-15).

(Isaiah 40:31) states those that wait upon the Lord shall remember their strength will be renewed. They shall mount up with wings-like Eagles, you shall run and not become weary, you will be able to walk and not grow tired.

When we receive His Son, we will be able to rejoice and understand why in times of need God said "He would hear you and not forsake you (41:17)."

(Isaiah 42:1) In order for us to be a servant of God, we must receive the guidance of the Holy Spirit. This guidance allows us to make decisions, which are pleasing to God according to His righteousness. As a servant, you realize your purpose here on Earth is to glorify your Father who resides in Heaven. He will not share His glory with graven images (42:8). Could it be possible, because of your need to grow spiritually you lack wisdom, knowledge, and understanding? Which causes you to choose disobedience and suffer the consequences? God is informing us of His ability to know things before they take place in (Isaiah 42:9). When we acknowledge He is our Lord and read (Isaiah 42:13-15). You will observe how He takes care of those who choose not to have a relationship with Him.

Then read verse (41:16) regarding those who have a personal relationship with Him. As long as we acknowledge suffering can be a result of sin. We will always remember to go to God in Jesus name. Humbly asking our Father who resides in Heaven is there anything. We forgot to ask forgiveness for which is causing our current situation. If the Holy Spirit reveals a "no", then we can be still acknowledging in time, we will be able to testify of God's "goodness and His mercy."

If the Holy Spirit reveals a "yes", stop what you are doing and begin to pray in Jesus' name, for the anointing of the Holy Spirit to reveal this or these situations. Then repent asking forgiveness in Jesus name with a sincere heart. Allow the glory of God and His righteousness to shine forth so others might desire to know Him as

How to Become Whole without the Better Half

their Lord and savior.

If we choose not to have a relationship with God in Jesus' name, we will be blind, we see but do not perceive. We hear but we do not really understand. There is a difference in spiritual guidance and being lead according to your flesh (Isaiah 42:20) (1 Corinthians 6:9-12, 15:35-58). Choosing a life outside the will of God is like seeing but not being able to observe and having ears open and still not hearing. This happens to those without a personal relationship with God in Jesus name. When we understand Jesus is our only redeemer, then we will mount up with wings like eagles in times of trouble. They go higher when others are after them. They arrive in apart of the atmosphere only they can soar in. Their enemies turn back in defeat. When the scripture says, "fear not for I am with thee" this reference is for those who have a personal relationship with the Father in Jesus' name.

When all His children have been taught of the Lord they will have great peace (Isaiah 54:13). He will provide for them and they shall not have fear as He put a protective hedge around you (Isaiah 54:14-17). Then we can say no weapon form against me shall prosper and

Lou Walker

everyone who speaks against me will not have success. This is the heritage of the servants of the Lord. When we incline our ears to the Lord and receive Him then our soul shall live and we will have an everlasting covenant with God just like David, (Isaiah 55:3).

Sabbath Day:

There is no excuse for not keeping a day available to assemble, honor, worship, and praise the living God. According to His words in (Jeremiah 17:19-27) the Sabbath must be kept. If Jesus could find time to reverence His Father who resides in Heaven, who are we?

As we choose to be obedient until Jesus returns acknowledging the Sabbath as the Lord's Day (Exodus 20:8-11). We will be blessed with medical science in this generation to save the life of others here on earth. We need to always glorify the living God whenever He performs a miracle in this day and time. Our faith and trust will always be renewed. Remembering to honor Him and doing things His way. Refusing to find pleasure for ourselves and speaking with the guidance of the Holy Spirit. Only then will we be able to receive God's blessing and favor according to His words (Isaiah 58:13-14).

We must acknowledge God has called a certain assembly of people. These people are His witnesses and servants. They will always know and believe every word He said is the truth. They have understood and they know there was no God before Him and there will not be a God after Him (Isaiah 44:6B). They also acknowledge He is Lord and savior (Isaiah 43:10-11). He still has people today; He has called into His righteousness. They realize they are a witness because He is Lord and savior according to verse 43:21. He said, "These people I formed for myself, they shall always praise Him." Those whom consider themselves wise without the guidance of the Holy Spirit. (Isaiah 44:25) speak of what happens to the wise man.

You must tell them.

Sometimes you listen and observe so many things outside the will of God until you become disillusioned. When you read, (Isaiah 45:8-13 and 19B) "I the Lord speak righteousness I declare things that are right." He reminds us in verse 22, "He is a just God, savior and there is no God besides Him." The day we choose to call upon Him we will be saved and all the ends of the Earth will know there is no one else besides Him. God said His words are righteousness and will not return, void. There will be a time when every knee shall bow and everyone confess: Jesus is Lord and savior. We need to tell the next generation and continue the process in future generations. When God speaks of remember the time of things of old for I am God. The world is moving at such a fast pace many will refuse to acknowledge, He is the living God and there is none like Him (Isaiah 50:7-8).

The nonbelievers will be worse than those in ancient times who chose not to believe. Anytime we have a relationship with the Father

Lou Walker

through His Son. The ability to observe things taking place around you becomes crystal clear. Does the future appear one where others will recall God and His righteousness? Will they remember He formed light and created darkness? He makes peace and create evil, because He can do all things. We need to start today writing, speaking and informing the next generation. He is Lord and savior and there is no other. If we do not surely, the words spoke in (Isaiah 47:10-15) was for our benefit of things to come. We can agree in the twenty-first century,that an education in the world is more important than obedience to God and seeking spiritual knowledge. We can also see the fruit of this knowledge by observing the many leaders who fell down without a crown at the feet of Jesus starting with Enron.

Those seeking counsel for anything should read what the scripture says about counseling from the wrong source. You will become confused and disillusion will exist among you (Isaiah 47:13). God continues to inform those who desire a life of obedience, can have a relationship with Him. "I am the Lord their God which teaches thee to profit and lead you the way you should go" (Isaiah 48:17). Sometimes you feel alone in this world. According to the words of God it shall be expected, just remember (Isaiah 49:23c) "thou shall not be ashamed that wait for me." Isaiah speaks of the servants suffering here on Earth for those who choose to wait on the Lord. The Lord Jesus Christ experience things said in (50:6) before man realized His purpose for being here on Earth.

If we really fear the Lord, we can be encouraged, He will provide for those who choose obedience. The scriptures state, "If you walk in darkness and hath no light? Let Him trust in the name of the Lord and stay upon His God" (50:10). This is why Jesus was wounded for our transgression and bruised for our iniquities. He has been chastised so we might have peace. We need to remember with His stripes you are healed in Jesus name, we appear as sheep without a shepherd without Christ. We **must** remember He paid the price with His life. He was oppressed and He was afflicted but He chose not to say a mumbling word. Remember these were God's plans for His Son. Jesus poured out His soul unto death and He was numbered with the transgressors. Jesus bares the sins of many, and makes intercession for the transgressor, (Isaiah 53:3-12).

When we choose sin over obedience to God,

Lou Walker

we need to remember it is our inadequacies and sin that has caused us the problems we are experiencing. It really is impossible to live a life of constant sinning and expect to have peace in the mist of your storms of life (1 John 3:5-10). God warned others regarding this same situation (Isaiah 59) "Thanks are unto God when He observes there was no man to intercede on their behalf until He sent His Son Jesus Christ." When the enemy shall come in like a flood the spirit of the Lord shall lift up a standard against him. We need to understand our deliverance will always be from God in the name of Jesus.

We need to remember during the wrath of God, when we can feel His hands of heaviness. He can still have mercy and show favor. David's story (2 Samuel 24:10) and his choices (24:12-15) and God's mercy (24:16) demonstrates His love for His child. When He has mercy in Jesus name remember it is possible to receive favor for your obedience to Him, (Psalm 57(all)). Jesus has come informing us of the spirit being upon Him. God has anointed Him to teach us and bind the broken hearted. Proclaim liberty because when the spirit of God sets you free you are free indeed. We must remember to glorify our Father with every step you take in freedom. Otherwise our freedom

How to Become Whole without the Better Half

will be short because we forgot our freedom came with a price. The blood Jesus shed way; back on cavalry it was the blood use to set us free.

Notes/Questions

Friends without Christ

The story about the two women in the book of (1 Kings 3:16-28) Solomon provides insight regarding friends with a disappearing friendship. They each had a baby about the same age; one of the women accidentally rolled on top of her baby and smothered it to death. In her distress, she remembers her friend who also had a baby the same age. Therefore, she enters where her friend is sleeping and lays the deceased baby beside her and takes the baby with life. When daylight appears the friend with the deceased baby realizes the child is not hers, she confronts her friend and she denies the deceased baby is her infant. These friends constantly disagree about the deceased infant until they must go before the judge who is Solomon, David's son, to render a judgment. The anointing of the Holy Spirit was imparted upon Solomon, because of David's relationship with God (1 Kings 3:14). When Solomon spoke, he had no prior knowledge regarding which of the ladies were telling the truth. He was in a position to make a decision without prior knowledge. Remember God promise about your seed and future generations who choose obedience will have the guidance of the Holy Spirit. The Spirit of God spoke through Solomon without Him having prior knowledge about the friends and their babies.

The way Solomon spoke caused the truth to come forth. He said, "Give me a sword; I will cut the living baby in half. Any true mother would give up the child rather than cause the child's death." One mother agreed yes, cut the child in half, the other mother said no, she could have the child. It did not take long for the Spirit of God to reveal the true mother, without man having prior knowledge. The Holy Spirit can always present the truth in all situations. Remember when you choose to become whole without the other half; you have a Father in Heaven waiting to restore the better half. This will be your relationship with Jesus, because the Father wants to put you back together again.

When you surrender to the living God in Jesus, name you will observe yourself as clay in the potter's hands. The potter would love to put you back together again. Which means your Father who resides in Heaven is waiting to heal the broken pieces and smooth the crack surfaces of your life (Isaiah 64:8).

If we do not have a relationship with Jesus Christ and the guidance of the Holy Spirit, we will be rebellious and shall be punished. We provoke anger continually in the face of the living God. Do you think God called your name? Did you choose not to answer? When He speaks you choose not to hear. Due to our disobedience, we choose evil before His eyes (Isaiah 65:12). We must remember the things He delights not in. Those who choose obedience will always have enough food to eat and shall drink and never become thirsty. We shall rejoice without any shame. We shall sing for joy of heart but shall cry for sorrow of the heart. We shall disagree loudly for vexation (cry in brokenness) of the Holy Spirit.

There are blessings for being obedient to the living God in Jesus name with the guidance of the Holy Spirit. Before you call on the name of Jesus, God will answer while you are speaking God will hear you (Isaiah 65:24).

Notes/Questions

God calls us into obedience to do His will:

When God called Jeremiah, He informed him of all that was planned before his arrival here on Earth. Sometimes we think things happen before God could inform us. This is not true God always knows what will be taking place. (My personal testimony of a confrontation being revealed in a dream, the night before the situation actually took place. This confirms God knowing all things in my personal experience). When all was said and done, I was too shocked to speak. I could only thank God for Jesus, His mercy and grace. We all can have this experience when we choose to accept Gods' only begotten Son Jesus Christ. Only then will we develop a relationship with our Father in Heaven.

When the Holy Spirit speaks through you, know there is power in the words of God (Jeremiah 1:8-10). Remember God always provide for His children, (Jeremiah 1:19).

Notes/Questions

Living Water

When, Jesus spoke to the woman at the well about drinking and never becoming thirsty again. This conversation was to help her recognize a problem she could not fix. In the book of (Jeremiah 2:13) He said because of the evils the people committed against the living God. They have forsaken Him; He is the fountain of living water. Which comes out of cisterns, but their cisterns cannot hold water because they are broken.

If Judah transgressed against God and He had to slay their children because they chose not to correct them. Do you think we can use this ex ample today, regarding our children who choose disobedience over the will of God? Do you think they can continually sin and be blessed (Jeremiah 2:30)?

Here is a warning for those who choose to be disobedient and refuse to accept the words of God. (Jeremiah 4:13, 22) "My people are foolish they have not known me, they are stupid children and have no understanding they are wise to do evil, but to do good they have no knowledge."

Does this sound like the children of today? They are so caught up in their friends who have no desire to follow the words of God. Yet they feel their knowledge is more advanced than past generations. Some have hardened their heart regarding God's words.

The foolish are poor when it comes to the words of God (Jeremiah 5:4). They are people without understanding, they have eyes but cannot see, and they have ears but cannot hear (Jeremiah 5:21). When we choose not to fear God out of honor, respect and tremble in His presence. This means you have forgotten who put the sand around the sea to keep water bound within its banks (Jeremiah 5:22).

It is obvious your heart is rebellious. You actually forgot He gives rain former and latter in His season. When we choose not to accept God's Son it is impossible to turn away from your sins. Only a sinner saved by grace, which the Lord has mercy on, has the guidance of the Holy Spirit provided by Jesus Christ. The spiritual guidance allows us to communicate with a Father who is

How to Become Whole without the Better Half

in Heaven, through His Son Jesus the mediator. Remember your iniquities (sins) have caused you not to receive things God desired, His child to receive in the name of Jesus (Jeremiah 5:25). Do you think God will lie stumbling blocks in front of those who choose disobedience and refuse their offering or sacrifices (Jeremiah 6:21)? He warned the people of Judah once before, are we any different?

Too much knowledge keeps you from being blessed, when pride slips into your life. Pride would be forced to keep its distance, if you remember these words **"If it had not been, for the Lord who was on my side, tell me where would I be."** Remember the wisest man that ever lived had to humble himself before God and acknowledge his existence without God in (1 Kings 3:7-9). Solomon states, "I am but a little child. I know not how to go out and come in." His speech pleased the Lord according to verse 10.

He warned the generations before us to obey "His voice and He will be their God and ye shall be my people and walk ye in all my ways that I have commanded you that it may be well unto you" (Jeremiah 7:23).

Lou Walker

There are many who have accepted Jesus as their personal Lord and savior experiencing mercy and grace. Do you think we are not instructed to live obedient to God's will? As children of God, we just have a helper in the anointing of the Holy Spirit to keep us going in the right direction. Remember Jesus is our mediator when we fail at obeying the words of God; should we sin without consequences? Should we expect God to answer prayer for those who choose to ignore His existence? Knowing they refuse to repent and change their ways? This action did not work for Judah. How are we different (Jeremiah 7:24)?

Is it possible for disobedience and the consequence to make you feel there is no balm in Gilead a physician there? Why then is the health of a love one not recovered (Jeremiah 8:22)?

What happens to a broken covenant? (Jeremiah 11:3-4) during the consequences of Israel, God cursed the man that refused to obey His words according to the covenant. We **must** remember the people of Israel, who refuse to follow Moses leadership and never made it into the promise land. God said obey my voice, and do all things according to my commandments. Obedience will allow Him to be our God and you to become His people. Do you think we can be disobedient in the twenty-first century? Just because Jesus is our Lord and savior, consequences for disobedience are still applied. Jesus can save us from our sins. Providing we accept Him and the guidance of the Holy Spirit. Spiritual guidance help the child of the living God choose to live like Christ in obedience to the words of God.

(Jeremiah 11:11) When, Israel and Judah broke God's covenant which He made with their fathers. God promised to bring evil upon them which they would not be able to escape and crying out to Him will not make a difference. We have Jesus as a mediator when we choose a relationship with the Father through His Son. We should not be deceived and think we can live in disobedience and not receive consequences for errors in judgment. Obedience produces blessing not disobedience. God actually warns others not to pray for these people nor cry for them. He said He would not hear them in the time that they cry unto me for their trouble (Jeremiah 11:14).

Sometimes when we are not on a certain level spiritually, there appear a need to question

Lou Walker

God's actions make sure you are in His will. Anytime we choose a life of obedience in Jesus' name. We can observe in (Jeremiah 12:1) how he asked questions of God and God chose to answer. For those who choose to live their life without Jesus Christ and think it's possible to be free of sin without the guidance of the Holy Spirit. We need to ask ourselves these questions: Can an Ethiopian change his skin color or leopards change their spots? Then those accustomed to do evil will do no good.

God can show favor to His children (Jeremiah 16:12-13). God is not pleased when man trust in man. Man will cause your heart to depart from God. "Blessed is the man who trust in God, and whose hope is in God" (Jeremiah 17:7).

How many of us know our hearts are deceitful above all things and desperately wicked? This is why, God searched our hearts and tried the reins; and gives to every man according to His ways and according to the fruit of His doings. (Jeremiah 17:9-10) reveals why it is necessary to have a relationship with Jesus, but without the guidance of the Holy Spirit, we would never have our hearts changed.

When we choose to be obedient to God according to His Son's words, we can reference the words in (Jeremiah 17:14) "Lord have mercy in Jesus name as you heal me and I know I am healed."

According to (Jeremiah 18:1-10) God reveals, how He remakes His children by using an example with Israel; all we need to do is repent and turn from things, which are displeasing to Him in Jesus' name.

For those who have experience leadership and guidance under any pastor, who chooses not to surrender to God in the name of Jesus? There is a message in (Jeremiah 23:1) regarding the consequences of the generations before the twenty-first century. God said "Woe be unto the pastors that destroy and scatter the sheep of my pasture." He reminds them, "He will visit upon them the evil of their doings." Always remember it is a blessing to teach the word of God. Providing you have the guidance of the Holy Spirit, but the Spirit will only guide you in Jesus name.

Notes/Questions

Warnings to God's People

It is very wrong for you to teach those who choose a relationship with God without Jesus. They cannot have the blessing of God in their disobedience. (Jeremiah 23:14-20) God reminds them as well as us today He has not sent these prophets yet than ran. Many are calling themselves prophets in this generation today. The warning provided in past generations still holds true today. "He said, He has not spoken to them, yet they prophesied." They also say these things in Jesus' name. You should know according to God's words things said then are being observed as the truth today. He will punish that man and his house. He said "every man's word should be their burden." For they have perverted the words of the living God. Do we do this in Jesus name in the twenty-first century? We have been warned to try the spirit by the spirits in (1 John 4:1-6).

If we are children of God because of our acceptance of Jesus according to (1 John 5:20-27). He warned Judah to turn away from evil in

Lou Walker

all things. So they might receive His blessing given to prior generations. In addition, they should not have any gods to serve or worship. We need to remember this provoked God to become angry with them. If they choose obedience with the works of their hands, He will cause them no harm (Jeremiah 25:5-6).

The consequences of sin can pass in time (Jeremiah 29:10-13). When, God allowed Babylon to control Jerusalem and Judah. They had position themselves in great disobedience. Hananiah interfered with the words God spoke to Jeremiah, deceiving Judah and Jerusalem causing his own death for his lies to the people. God promised His people after 70 years they could return to this place. He informed them they should call upon Him and pray. Then He will hear them when they sincerely seek Him. They will find Him with a sincere heart, (He will be found by them).

God reminds Israel in time He will break the yoke (bondage) He placed upon them. They must remember to serve Him and the one He shall raise up unto them meaning Jesus. As He has mercy, there will still be consequences for their disobedience (Jeremiah 30:8-11). As children of God, we also can be delivered from our sins. If we accept Jesus as Gods only begotten Son, we will be able to acknowledge God, as our Heavenly Father. Only through Jesus Christ will we receive our help in the guidance of the Holy Spirit. Then we can understand God's mercy and grace. Knowing we are forgiven but the consequences reminds us not to forget. As we choose a life obedience according to the will of God in Jesus' name. How many of us allow, our children to disrespect us and reward them for their disobedience? If we really love that child, we will not reward them but provide consequences to help them learn from their mistakes. According to the words of God if we spare the rod we spoil the child (Proverb 13:24). We should look around in this generation to see if the children are being spoiled. Some parents actually lock their bedroom doors fearing their own children while they sleep. We give them material things, to re place our guilt, for not being able to teach and train them according to the words of God.

They observe our mistakes using them to their advantage. They manipulate you without you realizing, they are taking advantage of the situation.

It is not their fault they are wise but weak according to the words of God.

If we do not apply consequences eventually they will receive greater consequences applied by God (Jeremiah 30:13-15).

As a child of God in the name of Jesus we will always understand. The sins of past generations only affect you, if you choose to live your life outside the will of God. We have consequences because we chose a life of disobedience. The disadvantage we place on our children is saying we have a relationship with God in Jesus' name. Then choose actions in life which are displeasing to God, this causes confusion within your children. The decisions our children make will cause more grief to the spirit than past generations. As we observe these present gods, we find they are more aggressive and controlling distractions. This causes the current generation to become more disobedient than you were in your generation. Therefore, they do not have consequences for your sins. They indulge in greater sins, but a life of obedience helps them realize, they can also choose a life of obedience and follow the will of God, (Jeremiah 31:29-30).

When we choose to accept Jesus as our personal Lord and savior, then we can understand better with the guidance of the Holy Spirit. When God said there is a day coming when you will not have to teach every man and his neighbor. "Do you know the Lord?" All will know Him from least to the greatest. As we receive His new covenant (Hebrews 9:15), His Son Jesus Christ. He will forgive our iniquity and remember our sins no longer. Only if we receive the guidance of the Holy Spirit, will we be allowed this freedom given unto you as a child of God (Jeremiah 31:33-34).

He told Israel after those days, "I will put my law in their inward parts and write it upon in their hearts. I will be their God and they shall be my people. As children of God in the name of Jesus, we are also His people."

God asked the question of Israel and it still applies today (Jeremiah 32:27) "Behold, I am the Lord the God of all flesh; is there anything too hard for me?" As children of God, we must have the answer to this question. Can we actually provoke God to become angry? According to (Jeremiah 32:29-30), Judah and Jerusalem was very capable and received consequences for their disobedience. As children of God, we should not grieve the Holy

Lou Walker

Spirit and provoke God to become angry, remember Jesus Christ is our mediator. He intercedes on our behalf asking God to have mercy on us but there must be consequences, if we are to learn and change our ways. God still reminds His children of His love after their consequences.

(Jeremiah 32:38-39) "And they shall be my people and I will be their God, I will give them one heart and one way that they may fear me forever, for the good of them and of their children after them." Until, we teach our children God is to be feared with, honor and respected. They will fail at being successful even in the twenty-first century. God made promises to Judah and Jerusalem of restoration after receiving consequences in His anger. He said "Behold I will bring health and cure, and will cure them and will reveal unto them the abundance of peace and truth." We can also receive these blessings in this generation providing we have a relationship with Jesus. (Jeremiah 33:5-9) reminds us when we harden our hearts regarding the words of God and follow the steps of past generations. Who chose not to follow God's word, we can look forward to God's promise to bring all the evil, He pronounced upon Judah and Jerusalem because

He also spoke to them. They refuse to hear, He called to them and they would not answer. Therefore, He said do certain things and these things they disobeyed. This provoked God to anger. We are a generation of people who also refuse to be obedient to the words of God. Do you think, we are provoking God to anger and calling on the name of Jesus in our disobedience, for God to bless our mess?

When Judah and Jerusalem refuse to be obedient and God reminded them of the abominable things that He hate. God reminds us of those who sinned before them and the consequences. They refuse to humble themselves so He finally set His face against them for evil and punish them by the sword, (Jeremiah 44:11, 13). They told Jeremiah regardless of what God speaks "through you we will not change our ways" (Jeremiah 44:16). Jeremiah reminds the people of the consequences of their sin in verse (44:23). This all took place because Judah and Jerusalem refuse to leave Egypt and turn from their wicked ways, which were displeasing to God.

God sent His Son, to teach us how to have a relationship with Him. Do you think this current generation is still doing wicked things, worshipping idols, and accepting abominations? Do we really think we can be disobedient to God's words without consequences in this day and time? Heaven forbid when we give excuses for not reading and following His guidance by the Holy Spirit. We must remember He sent His Son so we might live according to His words. Only with the guidance of the Holy Spirit, we will find ourselves capable of pleasing God in the name of Jesus.

If God reminded Judah and Jerusalem His word would stand during their disobedience (Jeremiah 44:28). God also punish them that they might know His words shall surely stand against their evil (Jeremiah 44:29). Exactly where do we have room for disregarding His words today? We should read about past generations mistakes, when it comes to disobeying God and adhere to their consequences. He allowed His Son to die for our sins, so we might have a spiritual relationship with a spiritual God. There seems to be a problem with this current generation understanding that is love. When Jesus was stretched out from side to side, they pierced His side to confirm He died; that is love. How many of us would consider giving up just one child for others sins? Not your sins but people you don't even know regardless of race, creed, or color. We just don't love others like that, but God sent His Son to die for each of us. He chose to be obedient even unto death for our sins.

Can we honestly say in this generation we are not sitting under the teaching of a shepherd who is leading us astray? (Jeremiah 50:6) speaks of God's people being lost sheep because the shepherd led them astray. Anytime God's calls us to surrender ourselves unto His will and we choose to lead our own lives, without surrendering and receiving the guidance of the Holy Spirit. We will always lead God's people astray. You are not capable of "Doing all things through Christ who strengthens you", according to (Philippians 4:13). Others who are not called into obedience will observe your disobedience and assume God; is not capable of following though with His words. This is one of the reasons you can lead others astray. They become confused being babes in Christ. We should always be mindful of those observing the children of God.

When God called Ezekiel into obedience, He gave him spiritual guidance to go before a rebellious nation, Israel, (Ezekiel 2:2, 3:14). He told Ezekiel he must receive His words within his

Lou Walker

heart and hear with his ears. God told him ahead of time what he would be dealing with in Israel. They would be impudent and hard-hearted (Ezekiel 3:7). God already has a word for those who chose to be rebellious. He dealt with rebellious Israel. His words to Ezekiel were to instruct them and the consequences for Ezekiel, if He chose not to speak according to His word (Ezekiel 3:16-21).

God also said they would put bands and bind him and he should not be among them (3:25). He should only speak when God speaks through him. Those that hearth let him hear, those who chose to forbear, let them forbear for they are rebellious (3:27). In today's generation, it is obvious if we don't know what the word of God says. We cannot stand according to His words so we fall for anything thus said man. (Ezekiel 8:15-18) States it is wrong for man to turn to the East and worship. This is a great abomination. He will not have pity regardless of the loud crying in His ears. Do we have a group today, who follow these steps of speaking to God without Jesus?

God made a promise to Israel regarding restoring and renewal after they suffered the consequence of disobedience (Ezekiel 11:4-12). He gave them one heart and a new spirit, removing their harden heart providing a heart of flesh. He provided this heart so they might be obedient to His will. Then He would be their God and they would be His people. Those who choose not to follow His guidance would have their consequences for their disobedience. Israel experience consequences and we are God's children because of our relationship with His Son. Shall we be free to choose disobedience in the twenty-first century without consequences? When Israel chose to be rebellious they had eyes but could not see, they had ears but could not hear. They were scattered among other nations without realizing what was happening to them (Ezekiel 12:14-15).

Those who are called into obedience, have a responsibility to teach others God's word or receive the consequences for refusing to enlighten others of their wickedness. God warned Israel and as children of God we need to warn others (Ezekiel 33:1-20). God gave His instructions on who shall lead and what shall be acceptable before Him. The destruction of the temple in (Matthew 24:1-3) speaks of the many who will be deceived, before Jesus returned to Earth. Always remember, God gives us an order for all things (Ephesians 5:22-33). Men shall fol-

Lou Walker

low Christ and women shall follow men **if they follow Jesus Christ** (1 Corinthians 11:3).

In (Ezekiel 44:23-24) the priests were to live according to God's plans for their life.
In their obedience, He gave them permission to teach and judge His people according to His laws. For this reason the Bible says (John 8:31-32) "And ye shall know the truth and the truth shall make you free." The Bible says if God is your Father in Heaven then you can hear God's words. (John 8:47) but a person who continues to sin against God does not hear the words of God. Remember God is a Spirit therefore only by the anointing of the Holy Spirit will the Spirit speak to you. Then you will be able to say "yes Lord to your will and my answer will be yes, Lord, yes."

The sheep follow the shepherd for they hear His voice and follow Him. Those who do not hear His voice are not capable of following the shepherd. Jesus is the shepherd and we are His sheep (John 10). He has come that we might have life because He gave His life for His sheep. We are warned in (John 10:26) those who refuse to believe are not His sheep. His sheep hear is voice and follow Him according to (John 10:27). They will not perish and it is impossible for man to take you out of the hands of God. God gave you to Jesus for safekeeping, the Father and Son being one. This is why you will have eternal life according to (John 10:28-30).

Notes/Questions

Mocking God

According to (Galatians 6:7) God said He would not be mocked. After accepting His Son Jesus and receiving the guidance of the Holy Spirit He has accepted us as sons and daughters. We are suppose to obey our Father who resides in Heaven. We need to acknowledge, the problem with having a Father in Heaven. He sees all things, hears all things, and knows everything even before we entered this world. He knew the decisions we were going to make. He formed us in our mother's womb knowing we would choose evil over good sometimes in this world. He has given us the ability to make choices in this world regardless of the situation. The problem occurs further when we choose the wrong road and appear to others we are on the right road. Others observe you as a Christian and think you are on a higher level spiritually. Which should be true if God has called you into obedience to do His will? It really is impossible for the blind to lead the blind. There is a blessing, if someone can see which directions you should follow. According to (Galatians 6:7) "Be not deceived, God will not be mocked whatsoever you sow that you shall reap." It is like a farmer who plants corn during the season and when it is harvested, he has corn. If God's word says do and we do not, then turn around and say "Lord it is still the same." We deceive ourselves and appear to be mocking God. Now if the words say do A+ and we do an A- or A, we appear to be trying to be obedient but we are falling short in Jesus' name. This shortness allows Jesus to intercede on our behalf to our Father in Heaven, to have mercy on us. We are struggling but we are trying to be obedient to His word. Once we observe God's mercy, we need to change our ways by repenting and finding time to grow spiritually. Then we can sing I am happy, happy in Jesus, because He is saving my soul and setting me free from my sins here on Earth. We can reference (Galatians 5:16-25) in these words you will find the wisdom of walking in the spirit and not walking in the flesh. Remember when I said the Bible is the blueprint of your life? You must follow the given instruction in order to be rebuilt and become whole again.

When, Ephraim chose a life outside the will of God. He reminded him He was the God from the land of Egypt and there should be no other

How to Become Whole without the Better Half

gods. They also needed to remember He is their savior. In the book of (Joel 1:3) he is told by God to tell the children and remind them to tell their children. Including the future generations of things, which took place according to the words of God? Joel warns them of the need to repent and a greater judgment day coming. He also tells the people God will send His Spirit before that great day. Those who have chose to receive His Son, now has access to the Holy Spirit. This is why you must believe in the **birth** (Matthew 1: 24-25, Luke 2:1-7), **life** (the four gospels Matthew, Mark, Luke and John), **death** (Matthew 27: 51-56, Mark 15:38-41, Luke 23:45, 47-49), **resurrection** (1 Corinthians 15, Luke 24:1-48) and **ascension** (Mark 16:19-20, Luke 24:49-53) **of Jesus Christ the Son of the living God.**

The people were also reminded if they turn their heart to God. He is gracious and merciful, slow to anger, great kindness and repented him of evil. It shall come to pass "whosoever shall call on the name of the Lord shall be delivered (Joel 2:32)." How many of us can actually testify, because you call on the name of Jesus in a time of trouble. He heard and answered your prayer right away. For example, I stopped at a red light and someone was coming very fast behind me. He would have total my vehicle un-

Lou Walker

til I said, "Lord have mercy", then the driver turned away very fast almost turning over his own vehicle. This was a prayer being answered instantly.

When, you have a personal relationship with God through His Son Jesus. We can actually say we are strong in the name of Jesus. God has supplied you with the Holy Spirit through His Son Jesus. You really can do all things through Christ who strengthens you (Philippians 4:13). In this generation, we are choosing to be disobedient and still thinking we can please God in Jesus' name. God warned the people in (Zephaniah 1:12) "That say in their hearts, the Lord will not do well neither will He do evil." Why do you think the scripture speaks of the afflicted and poor being able to trust God? Could it be possible they don't have any idols to distract them from who God really is, **"He said I am that I am?"**

When God told Haggai to tell the people to consider your ways in (1:5) the message still holds true today. We need to stop and consider our ways. We deceive ourselves if we think we can take God's love and compassion for granted in this generation. He has provided away for us to turn away from things displeasing to Him (Romans 6 (all)). Heaven help those who take His love for granted your consequences will be a reminder of His Holiness. We have sown much but have little to show, we eat but we are still hungry, then we drink but are still thirsty. We can have on clothes but still be cold. Look at the money you have but you are always robbing Peter to pay Paul. It is like having a bag of money with holes in the bottom. It comes in but it goes out very quickly. This is why we need to consider our ways even in today's generation.

There was a time during Zechariah (7:12-13) when the people chose disobedience over the words of God. As the man of God cried for them to change their ways, they ignored Him. Then God turned a deaf ear and would not hear them in times of trouble.

Anytime we are not grounded in our faith and belief in the Father, Son, and the Holy Spirit (Matthew 13:18-23). We are like Isaiah said, "Ye hypocrites", we favor traditions over the words of God. The people come close but they refuse to know Him personally. We say things; we worship the teachings and doctrine of man because we do not know for ourselves what the words of God really say. (Matthew 15:7-9) God

Lou Walker

says if a man desires a woman, he must marry her (1 Corinthians 7:9). In the twenty-first century we follow the wisdom of the world and recommend the two live together without a marriage covenant with God, then we expect God to bless our mess (Mark 7:6-9).

Jesus' teaching on divorce according to (Mark 10:5-12) "From the beginning of creation God made them male and female." In the twenty-first century we have accepted male and male or female and female relationships read (Leviticus 18:22, 20:13). Do not be confused before we were born men desired other men in Sodom and Gomorrah. When God became tired of their disobedience, He just removed them off the face of the Earth (Genesis 19:5-7, 24-25). Do you think you need to be praying today asking God to have mercy on America in Jesus' name? We are heading in the wrong direction accepting marriages of the same gender. God said, "I am that I am" we have come into this world changing His original design (Genesis 1:26-28). A marriage covenant without the guidance of the Holy Spirit is a guaranteed to fail, between a male and female. How can we begin to justify marriage of the same gender being blessed? (Luke 16:15) God observes the heart of man. Things highly praised among us are usually an abomination in the sight of God. As we make the choices God will make the decisions.

Now that I have your attention, when was the last time you receive an invitation to a gathering. You could invite as many guests as you would like. Allow me to invite you and others to (Matthew 11:28-30). I am also looking forward to that great day; Jesus is getting us ready for that great day.

Notes/Questions

While I'm on this road Lord will you guide me?

Lord, teach me to watch, fight and pray (1 John 5 (all)). I realize the saints of old tried to lay a path for future generations. We are successful sometimes but we are falling short often in this generation with all the distractions available to us.

The day you decided to come as an example of how to live a life of obedience was a blessing to us. We acknowledge you have created us in your image. Design with a plan and purpose to know you personally. We thank you for the blueprint your words the Bible. Which reveals answers to questions, we have for a successful life here on earth.

We really are grateful for past generation's mistakes. We realize you are Holy, Righteous and a Spirit. Your love and compassion is greatly appreciated among your children here on earth. We understand those who do not know you are without the guidance of the Holy Spirit, who

Lou Walker

provides wisdom, knowledge and understanding in all things (Romans 8(all)).

Hopefully they will **ask somebody** about your Son Jesus Christ so they will come to know you personally and have an abundant life.

Thank you for the **victory of Becoming Whole without the Better Half** in the name of JESUS.

Printed in the United States
102941LV00003B/118/A